WhOSe ZOo?

pictures by orlie Jensen

story by JAMES S. KERR

AUGSBURG PUBLISHING HOUSE
Minneapolis 15, Minnesota

WHOSE ZOO?

We're going to look at animals to see if we can find
The persons in the Bible that these friends call to mind.
Now when they're all together and we know who is who,
We'll have a whole collection we'll call our Bible zoo!

First view the picture carefully and read the verse below,
The answer is a Bible tale that all of us should know.
Now if you don't remember who, or where, or what,
    or when –
Just turn the page and you can read the story once again!

THE RAM

The ram is quite proud, you can tell by his walk,
As he struts on ahead up in front of the flock.
In contests of butting he seldom is bested!
Now whom do we think of, a man that God tested?
Who?

Abraham

Abraham was chosen by God to be the father of a great nation. Yet Abraham was one hundred years old before his son Isaac was born.

Abraham loved Isaac very much. Yet when God told Abraham to build an altar on a mountain and sacrifice Isaac, Abraham obeyed. He saddled his donkey and took his son to the mountain. There Abraham and Isaac built an altar. God had tested Abraham, and Abraham was faithful.

Then God showed Abraham a ram that was caught by its horns in the bushes. And the ram was sacrificed instead of Isaac.

Because Abraham was faithful and had obeyed God he was greatly blessed.

Based on Genesis 22

THE GREAT FISH

It's a whale of a tale
    of a ship that was followed
And a man overboard
    that a fish promptly swallowed.
Why the fish didn't keep
    the man is a question
Of the planning of God,
    and *not* indigestion!
Who?

Jonah

Jonah was a frightened man! God had called him to preach in the wicked city of Nineveh. Jonah did not think that the people of Nineveh deserved to hear God's word. So Jonah tried to run away on a ship bound for Spain.

God knew very well where Jonah was and sent a great storm to toss the ship. It was a terrible storm. Jonah knew that God caused the storm because God was angry with him for running away. Jonah told the sailors to throw him over the side of the ship and God would stop the storm. There seemed to be no other way to quiet the storm. So the sailors tossed Jonah overboard.

But Jonah did not drown. God had prepared a great fish to swallow Jonah alive. Three days and nights later the fish spat out Jonah on dry land. And this time Jonah did as God told him to do.

Based on the Book of Jonah

SEVEN COWS

Seven cows so very fat
They hardly got to where they're at!
And seven cows so very lean
It makes you wonder where they've been!
Who?

Joseph

Joseph had been sold into slavery in Egypt by his brothers. And in Egypt Joseph was put in prison for something he did not do. God told Joseph the meanings of dreams. And Joseph began telling some prisoners what their dreams meant.

The Pharaoh heard of this and sent for Joseph. The Pharaoh had some dreams that no one in the whole country could explain. The dreams were about seven fat cows and seven lean cows. Joseph told the Pharaoh that the seven fat cows meant seven good harvests. The seven lean cows meant seven years of bad harvests.

The Pharaoh was very much impressed by Joseph's knowledge. He placed Joseph in charge of storing the grain from the good harvests, and selling it in bad years. And Joseph was made a prince over all the land.

Based on Genesis 41

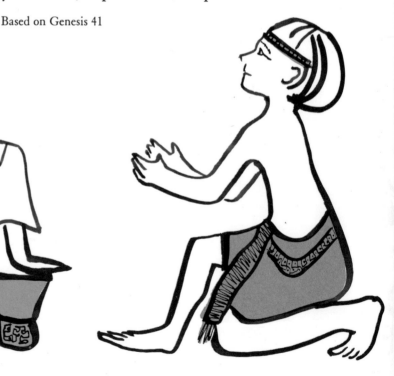

SHEEP

Sheep and a shepherd, harp and a king,
Poems of praise that we still sing.
Sheep out a-grazing, knee-deep in clover,
Oil for anointing, the cup running over;
Sheep in the valley in search of cool water,
A battle to fight, a giant to slaughter;
Sheep led and protected by staff and by rod
Should tell you the name of this man of God.
Who?

David

When David was still a young shepherd boy he met the great giant Goliath on the battlefield. David had only a sling and a stone, but he also had God with him. David's aim was true and the giant Goliath died. The army of the Philistines turned and ran.

As God had told him when he was only a boy, David became king of Israel. He was also a great soldier. His army captured Jerusalem, and it became known as "the city of David." David planned to build a great temple in Jerusalem. He chose the site and made the plans. But David spent so much time in battle that the temple was not built until Solomon became king.

David, the great soldier, was also a great musician. He wrote the Psalms and music for the temple choirs. David was king for forty years.

Based on 1 and 2 Samuel

THE RAVEN

The raven from its haven,
   to places far off sped,
To Cherith brook twice daily took
   a meal of meat and bread.
For in God's plan there was a man
   who waited there alone,
He daily prayed, God's will obeyed,
   until the drought was gone.
Who?

Elijah

Elijah was a fearless prophet. God told him that if the people did not obey the commandments there would be no rain for three years. When Elijah told the king, he became angry and tried to kill Elijah. But Elijah escaped to a brook called Cherith.

For nearly three years Elijah lived by Cherith brook. God sent ravens to carry meat and bread to Elijah every day.

When the rains came again Elijah went out again to the people preaching God's Word.

Based on 1 Kings 17

THE ANIMAL PARADE

Now here's an easy one for you,
Animals marching, two by two!
Remember him? He had his own zoo!
Who?

Noah

The people laughed at Noah. Men just didn't build such big ships so far from the water! They said it was much too big to move. It was much too big for his family! But Noah was doing what God had told him. The people also laughed when he told them of the flood God would send.

But the flood did come. For forty days and forty nights the rains poured down. Noah had placed two of every kind of animal and all his family in the ark with him as God had said to do. The water not only floated the ship, but took it far away.

Finally the water went down, and the animals and Noah and his family could come out of the ark. The first thing that Noah did was to build an altar to thank God for saving them from the flood.

Based on Genesis 6-9

THE LION

Here is the lion, prowling, proud,
His head is high, his roar is loud.
A copper-colored coat and mane
Make him very, very vain.
The king of beasts he's often named,
So fierce and ruthless, seldom tamed—
Yet harm one man he did not dare,
Though thrown right in the lions' lair . . .
Who?

29771 dh

Daniel

Daniel was an honest man. But he had enemies who wanted to get rid of him. Daniel's enemies knew that three times every day Daniel prayed to God.

So the enemies went to king Darius. "Make a law," they said. "Make it against the law to pray to anyone but the king."

Foolishly the king agreed. The law was made, and whoever broke it would be locked in the lions' den.

Daniel's enemies quickly told the king that Daniel was praying to God, and not to the king. The king had no choice but to lock Daniel in the lions' den.

All night the king did not sleep. For Daniel was his friend. In the morning the king rushed out to find out if Daniel was alive.

"God sent his angels to close the lions' mouths," Daniel told the king. "I am not harmed." Then the king knew that Daniel's enemies had wanted the new law only to get rid of Daniel.

So the king said, "Let the enemies of Daniel be thrown to the lions, all those who accused him! And let all men worship the God of Daniel!"

Based on Daniel 6

THE CAMEL

Now this is a camel, a dromedary,
All manner of things he's made to carry.
When saddled he makes a good beast to ride,
Though he's ugly and stubborn and quite full of pride.
He's the "ship of the desert," some people say,
He can go without water for many a day:
Which doesn't mean much to you or to me,
But whom do we think of when we mention three?
Who?

The Wise Men

With gifts of frankincense, gold and myrrh, the wise men came from the East to worship baby Jesus. They had seen his bright star and followed it over many lands. They traveled by camel caravan over mountains, across deserts, and through valleys.

King Herod asked the wise men to show him the place where baby Jesus lived. But the wise men knew that Herod wanted to kill Jesus. The wise men left by another way so Herod would not know where Jesus was. But Herod searched with his army for the Christ-child.

Joseph and Mary and Jesus escaped to Egypt. There they lived until Herod died and it was safe to come home again.

Based on Matthew 2

THE PIG

A whole herd of pigs in a great squealing huddle,
Snorting and rolling in every large puddle;
Pushing and shoving, with manners the crudest!
It seems they are trying to be just the rudest!

They don't seem to care much or see what they eat,
And often they stand in their food with their feet!
Now whom do we think of, who ran away
And ate with the pigs for many a day?
Who?

The Prodigal Son

Jesus told the parable (story) of a man with two sons. The youngest son asked his father for a share of all that was his so that he could go out and live his own way.

The young son went far away. But he spent his money foolishly. He did not work to earn more money, and soon all that he had was spent. Times were very hard and there was little to eat. Finally the young son had to go to work. But the only job he could find was feeding pigs. And the only food was the food the pigs ate.

The young son knew that his father's servants lived better than that. So the young son decided to go home and ask his father to forgive him. Perhaps his father would let him be a servant on his own farm! That would be better than eating with pigs.

The father ran to meet his young son, and forgave him. And the father prepared a great feast and celebration to welcome his son home.

Based on Luke 15:11

THE DONKEY

He's funny, but cute,
    and his ears are long,
He's small, it's true,
    but he's very strong.
A donkey's quite stubborn,
    in fact downright mulish!
He sounds and he acts
    in some ways that are foolish.
But one time quite proudly
    he carried a king,
The crowds gathered round
    "hallelujahs" to sing....

Who?

Jesus

Jesus was coming into Jerusalem! There was great excitement everywhere. The people went about waving palm branches, and calling Jesus the "king of Israel." The road was covered with palm branches and even with coats and robes.

The people of Israel wanted Jesus to be a great king. They wanted him to take the throne and rule like other kings. They did not yet understand that Jesus talked about the kingdom of heaven.

Jesus did not enter Jerusalem with a great army, as other kings would have done. Instead, he rode in on a young donkey.

"Hosannah," the crowds cried. "Jesus, king of Israel," they cried. And none of them really knew how great a king he was.

Based on John 12:12

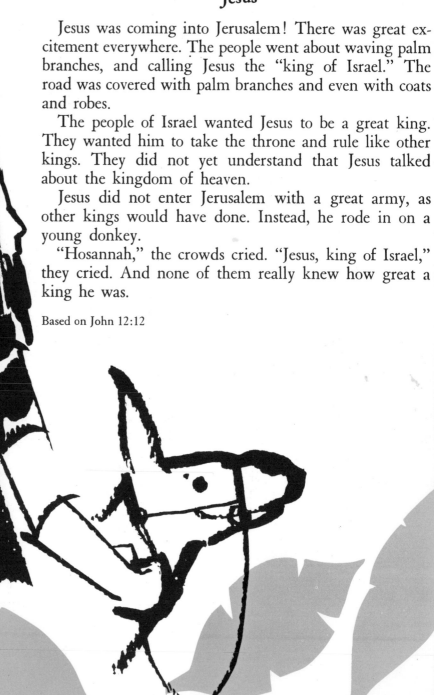

These animals you've seen before,
    as you were paging through,
And now they're all together
    in our Bible zoo.
Each is for a man we met
    while traveling through this book,
Now take a little memory test
    and name them in one look.

Date Due

PRINTED IN U. S. A.